Living Between The Advents

Preaching Advent In Year B

Michael L. Ruffin

CSS Publishing Company, Inc., Lima, Ohio

LIVING BETWEEN THE ADVENTS

Copyright © 2005 by
CSS Publishing Company, Inc.
Lima, Ohio

All rights reserved. No part of this publication may be reproduced in any manner whatsoever without the prior permission of the publisher, except in the case of brief quotations embodied in critical articles and reviews. Inquiries should be addressed to: Permissions, CSS Publishing Company, Inc., P.O. Box 4503, Lima, Ohio 45802-4503.

Scripture quotations are from the New Revised Standard Version of the Bible, copyright 1989 by the Division of Christian Education of the National Council of the Churches of Christ in the USA. Used by permission.

Brief excerpts from p. 44 of PECULIAR TREASURES: A BIBLICAL WHO'S WHO by Frederick Buechner, copyright © 1979 by Frederick Buechner. Illustration copyright © 1979 by Katharine A. Buechner. Reprinted by permission of HarperCollins Publisher, Inc.

Library of Congress Cataloging-in-Publication Data

Ruffin, Michael Lee, 1958-
Living between the Advents : preaching Advent in Year B / Michael L. Ruffin.
  p. cm.
ISBN 0-7880-2379-9 (perfect bound : alk,. paper)
1. Advent sermons. 2. Baptists—Sermons. 3. Sermons, American—21st century, 4. Common lectionary (192). Year B. 5. Christian life—Baptist authors. I. Title.

BV4254.5.R84 2005
252'.612—dc22

2005015580

For more information about CSS Publishing Company resources, visit our website at www.csspub.com or e-mail us at custserv@csspub.com or call (800) 241-4056.

Cover design by Barbara Spencer
ISBN 0-7880-2379-9   PRINTED IN U.S.A.

*For Joshua and Sara,
our children*

Table Of Contents

Preface — 7

Part One: Living Between The Advents
- Anticipation — 11
- Assurance — 16
- Testimony — 21
- Fulfillment — 26
- Endnotes — 31

Part Two: While We Wait
- Watching And Working — 35
- Taking Advantage Of The Opportunity — 41
- On Being Safe And Sound — 47
- Trusting God's Promises — 53
- Endnotes — 58

Part Three: Advent Imperatives
- Watch! — 61
- Repent! — 65
- Rejoice! — 69
- Worship! — 73
- Endnotes — 76

Preface

A year passes from Christmas to Christmas, but it seems like a much shorter time. A week passes from Sunday to Sunday, but that seems like a much shorter time, too. More than 2,000 years have passed since the First Advent. That seems like a long time to us, but on God's calendar, I suppose it really isn't. We who are Christians find ourselves living between the First and Second Advents of Christ and as we do so we find ourselves living from one day to the next, from one week to the next, from one year to the next. These sermons, I hope, will provide both comfort and challenge for those who are doing their best to live as disciples of Jesus in these days. I hope that they will also assist preachers who are always on the lookout for a line of reasoning, an illustration, an observation, or just a phrase to enliven the imagination.

The sermons in this book were originally written to be preached and all of them have been preached. They enter a new stage of life here, but I trust that their oral nature comes through. I also hope that even in print they reflect the interplay between preacher, text, Spirit, and congregation that produced them.

Advent was never mentioned in the beloved church in which I was raised. Christmas worship for us was the Christmas play, a visit by Santa Claus, and maybe one sermon about the baby Jesus. Somewhere during my journey, I was introduced to Advent worship and my life has been greatly enriched by sharing with all the saints in this season of celebration, repentance, and anticipation. Together we find ourselves praying, listening, trusting, and trying, so that we might be found faithful to the one who came, who comes, and who will come. Even so, come, Lord Jesus.

Michael L. Ruffin

Part One

Living Between The Advents

Anticipation

Mark 13:32-27

To say that to live between the advents is to live in anticipation is really redundant. In essence, Advent *is* anticipation. The word "Advent" means "coming" or "arrival." The day on which Christ was born marked his arrival and fulfilled the anticipation or hope of those who were anticipating and hoping for him to come; it did, at least, if they had "eyes to see and ears to hear." But before he came there was anticipation; there was longing. The celebration of Advent is all about anticipation and longing as we look for the Christ Child to come to us in a new way.

Christ has already been born, of course. He was born to the Virgin Mary and to her gracious husband, Joseph, in a stable or cave in David's city, Bethlehem. There, Mary "wrapped him in bands of cloth, and laid him in a manger" (Luke 2:7). All of this happened in 4 B.C.E., which was over 2,000 years ago! So why do we observe Advent as a time of anticipation, since the event that we are anticipating has already occurred?

We do so, in the first place, because we are anticipating the arrival of Christ in our lives in a new way. Some of you are wrestling with the conviction you have from the Holy Spirit that you should accept Christ as your Savior and become a child of God. We anticipate that Advent will be a time when Jesus will become very real to you and that you will not let Christmas pass without accepting the Savior who was born on that day.

Others of us are already Christians and we cannot become Christians "again." But my experience has been that we can encounter Christ in a manner that will shed new light on our relationship with him. We are not like the little girl who was sitting in the floor, drawing a picture. Her father said to her, "What are you drawing, honey?" She replied, "I'm drawing a picture of God." "But no one knows what God looks like," her father protested. "They will when I'm finished," she answered.[1] We cannot presume to know all that we can know about Jesus. We do not know him well enough. Nor can we presume to know all that there is to know about Jesus. So we anticipate experiencing Christ in a new way.

We observe Advent in the second place because of our anticipation of the Second Coming of Christ. Our Bibles teach us that the baby Jesus was the Messiah and that he fulfilled that role by being perfectly obedient to the will of God even to the point of giving his own life on the cross. He then rose from the dead on the third day. Now he sits at the right hand of the Father, awaiting the day when he will come in power to bring the kingdom of God in its fullness. That is the event which today's scripture anticipates. That is the event which we anticipate. That is the event of which the event of Christmas reminds us and assures us. He came, and he will come!

So Advent is all about anticipation. We anticipate the coming of Christ into our lives for the first time or in a new way, and we anticipate his Second Coming. But how do we anticipate the coming of Christ? We can learn from those who anticipated encountering him in his First Advent.

First, we can *look for his coming*. Our model here is Simeon. When Jesus was about forty days old, Mary and Joseph took him to Jerusalem to present him to the Lord (see Leviticus 12:2-8 for the pertinent law). There they met Simeon. Luke tells us that "it had been revealed to him by the Holy Spirit that he would not see death before he had seen the Lord's Messiah" (2:26). And when he saw the baby Jesus he took him in his arms and said, "Master, now you are dismissing your servant in peace, according to your word; for my eyes have seen your salvation, which you have prepared in the presence of all peoples; a light for revelation to the Gentiles and for glory to your people Israel" (2:29-32). So Simeon was actively looking for the coming of Christ.

Are we actively looking for his coming? Do we want to see him; do we want to experience him? Are we living as if we are looking for his return? The baby Jesus grew up to be the teacher Jesus and one day he told his disciples, "Beware, keep alert, for you do not know when the time will come. It is like a man going on a journey, when he leaves home and puts his slaves in charge, each with his work, and commands the doorkeeper to be on the watch" (Mark 13:33-34). We anticipate his coming by looking for it; we look for it by performing the ministry that Jesus left for us to do.

Second, we can *see the signs of his coming*. Our models here are the Wise Men. You will remember that those Persian astronomers came to Herod and said, "Where is the child who has been born king of the Jews? For we observed his star at its rising, and have come to pay him homage" (Matthew 2:2). They had seen the sign of the coming of Jesus, and they had acted upon what they had seen, launching a search for the child. It is interesting that these were "foreigners" who would not be expected to see the sign; they are to be contrasted with those we meet in the gospels who should have seen the signs but did not. There is an implicit warning here for those of us who are the "insiders": we need to be watchful.

Just before Jesus told his disciples to watch for his coming, he spoke to them of "signs." The signs of which he spoke are really signs of tribulation and difficulty. Whenever we talk about such signs, people tend to associate the words with some present crisis, especially if one is occurring in the Middle East, and when is that not the case? Perhaps you are wondering if such events constitute a sign of the impending return of Christ.

I think that William Lane is right when he says that in this chapter there is a difference between the things that the signs signify and the Second Coming of Christ.[2] Look again at what Jesus says in Mark 13. Throughout the bulk of the chapter, Jesus is talking about the fall of Jerusalem to the Romans in 70 C.E. He is speaking of a historical event that in his time was yet to occur and that in our time has already occurred. That fall was one of the signs that the end was near, and that happened almost 2,000 years ago!

His followers could (and can) see the signs (v. 30) but we cannot know when Jesus will come (v. 32).[3] Our call is to be watchful and ready. Thus, we must say that what is happening now probably is a sign of his impending coming, even as many other events over the last two millennia have been signs of his impending coming. Is he near? Yes. How near? We cannot know. Still, we need to understand that he is coming, and be sensitive to the indicators, and work in light of them.

Third, we can *hear the word of his coming*. Again, we look for models, and we find good ones in the shepherds. The shepherds on the hills outside Bethlehem heard the word of the Messiah's birth proclaimed by the heavenly host. In response, they went to see the baby in the manger. It was good news, and they recognized it as such.

We can anticipate his coming as we hear the word of his coming. Now, you may say, "Well, if I heard it from a bunch of angels, I'd believe it, too." You may not hear it from angels, but listen: the word proclaimed by the angels is the same word proclaimed today by the Bible, by the church, and by the Holy Spirit, and it is just as powerful. Will you hear the good news about his First Advent and his Second Advent and respond to it?

We can sum up all that we have said by saying two things.

First, we can anticipate the coming of Jesus with anxiousness — out of love. Mark Galli wrote of the fervor with which the German reformer, Martin Luther, and the early American preacher, Jonathan Edwards, anticipated the Second Coming. Galli compared their attitude with the longing with which one in love anticipates the return of his loved one from a long trip.[4] Should we not be anxious for the return of Jesus if for no other reason than that we love him? Should we not want to experience him anew if for no other reason than that we love him?

Second, we can anticipate the coming of Jesus with action — out of vigilance. To anticipate the coming of Jesus in new ways or in his Second Advent is not to sit around speculating about dates or times nor about the manner in which he will come. To anticipate his coming is to do his will, which means performing the ministry to which he has called us. It is to be faithful to the calling we have under Christ to live lives of self-giving devotion and of willingness to endure persecution. To "watch" is to do our jobs as Christians.

The story is told of Henry III, king of Bavaria in the eleventh century. Growing tired of his duties, Henry went to a local monastery and presented himself to the prior (the fellow in charge of the monastery), intending to live out his life in quiet contemplation. "Your majesty, do you understand that this is about obedience? Whatever I tell you under authority you must do," the prior said. Henry answered, "Yes, father, I understand." So the prior said, "Then, your majesty, in obedience to me, go back to your throne and serve in the place God has put you."[5]

As we live between the Advents, let us properly anticipate the coming of our Lord. Let us submit ourselves to his will and then do his will as we actively await his coming.

Assurance

Psalm 85

We live our lives suspended somewhere between a period and an ellipsis. What has already happened is a completed sentence, the end of which is marked by that grammatical mark of finality, the period. What is happening now is not finished, so we cannot know how it will turn out. The present is a sentence which trails off into a series of periods — an ellipsis. That ellipsis also indicates that there is a future; there is something else out there. We do not, however, know exactly what that is.

So we live between a period and an ellipsis, between a completed past and a continuing present, facing an uncertain future.

Such is true for all people, but it is doubly true for the person who professes faith in Christ and trust in God. Why? Because we live in *our* present between *our* past and *our* future, but we also live in *God*'s present between *God*'s past and *God*'s future.

We could talk about the latter half of that statement for a long time, but I want to restrict it thusly: By "God's past" I mean the First Advent of Jesus Christ; by "God's future" I mean the Second Advent of Jesus Christ; by "God's present" I mean whatever events are happening now in the lives of believers. Obviously, for the Christian, our present and God's present intersect. The present is the present, after all. Also, our past is informed by God's past, and our future is assured by God's future. We can live between the Advents with assurance regarding the future.

Psalm 85 is about living between the past and the future. It is about knowledge, need, and assurance, and it reminds us that what we know from the past helps us in the present because it assures us concerning the future.

What We Know From The Past (vv. 1-3)

If you are a Christian, then you know from your past experience what God will do for you. You also know that he has done what he has done in response to who you have been and to what you have done. In other words, he has done what he has done out of his grace.

We Know That We Have Been Sinners Under The Judgment Of God

I once watched a documentary on the Beatles. It was amazing to see how much the members of the group changed from 1964, when they first came to the United States, until 1970, when they disbanded. You would hardly have known they were the same people. When I see old photographs of myself, I can scarcely believe that those pictures are of me. What I was seems so far removed from what I am.

So it is when we look back on our lives when we lived them apart from God and under the judgment of God. We can scarcely believe it, but there we were. Like the psalmist looks back and remembers a time when the people and the land were under the judgment of God because of sin, so do we remember what it was like to live apart from God.

We Know That God Has Acted To Forgive And To Restore Us

The psalmist knew. He remembered that in the past God had forgiven the sin of the people and had brought restoration to their land. He knew that God had withdrawn his judgment when the people turned back to him.

Can we not look back and see that God has acted to forgive and to restore us, too? When did he do so?

In the birth, life, death, and resurrection of Jesus. The world was living apart from God, seemingly unable to comprehend his desires and demands despite his efforts to communicate them through the Hebrew people and the events and words of the Old Testament. So what did he do? He acted, and he acted decisively and definitively. He acted to forgive people and to bring people into a relationship with himself by the sending of his only Son. His Son entered the world at Bethlehem and departed it from

Jerusalem. That is what happened; we can read it in the Bible and we can experience it in our hearts.

In the coming of Christ into our own lives. We know what God has done through Christ because we read it in the Bible and we believe it; we know what God has done through Christ in our own lives because we have experienced it. God went to all that trouble to send his Son into the world but he did it so that his Son could come into our hearts. When you experience something like that, you know it.

What do we know from the past? We know that we have been sinners who lived apart from God but we also know that God has worked in history and in our lives to bring us into relationship with his Son. He is in our hearts because of what has happened. But what is happening now? What do we need now?

What We Need In The Present (vv. 4-7)

We live against the backdrop of the past, but we do not live in the past. We live knowing what God has done in the past, but we live needing help in the present.

Such was the situation that this psalm addressed. The writer knew that God had helped his people in the past, but they needed help again, *now!* The people had sinned again, and they needed deliverance, again. They fell under the judgment of God again, and they needed to be liberated, again.

I do not really want to address you with the assumption that you are "backslidden," to use a term I heard a lot growing up. But I know that many times in my present I discover that I have sinned again, or that I am standing under the judgment of God again. So, when we are Christians and we have experienced God's salvation but we have harmed our relationship with him, what do we need?

We Need Restoration
We need restoration because we continue to violate our relationship with God and in so doing we harm ourselves. We go against his will. We have "other gods before him." We choose to do things

our way rather than his way. We ignore the teachings of his word. When that happens, we need to experience God's restoring power, and because he has restored us before, we know that he will restore us again.

We Need An Exhibition

The psalmist wrote, "Show us your steadfast love, O LORD, and grant us your salvation" (v. 7). When we sin, when we harm our relationship with God, we need an exhibition of God's grace, of his faithful love toward us. We can be sure that he will show us his love and grace when, like the psalmist, we recognize our need for it.

These two things, a restoration of your relationship with God and an exhibition of God's faithful love, may be experiences of which you find yourself in need today. You may sense your sin; you may feel yourself to be standing under God's judgment; you may be seeking a way out. To God is where you must turn in hope, because he has helped you before. He sent Jesus; he saved you. He will help you again — now!

What We Know For The Future (vv. 8-13)

We have said that we know what God has done in the past because of his Word and because of our experience. That knowledge enables us to have hope in the present, in this time between the Advents, when we sin and need forgiveness and restoration. We can also have assurance for the future, even though we cannot see it. This assurance is based on the promises of God.

The Promise Of Peace

"He will speak peace to his people, to his faithful ..." (v. 8). "Peace" here is *shalom*, that state of well-being that proceeds from a sound relationship with God. There will be peace in our lives when the relationship we have with God is sound and secure. This peace is made possible by the First Advent of Christ; it will culminate in the Second Advent of Christ. We can know that a great day of peace for God's people is coming. We can be sure of it because God has promised it.

The Promise Of Presence

The word from the Lord to his longing people was, "Surely his salvation is at hand for those who fear him, that his glory may dwell in our land" (v. 9). Here, as in many other places in the Bible, "glory" is a synonym for "presence." For the glory of the Lord to be present is for the Lord to be present. In the future, God promises to come be with his people.

What a day it will be! Jesus Christ will come again and fully establish the reign of God in the world! But remember, he has already come — the proof is already there, and remember, he is already present in our lives through the Holy Spirit, who is the signifier to us of our salvation. We are assured by his promise of his future presence.

The Promise Of Productivity

The psalmist paints a glorious picture of a future for his people when everything will be as it ought to be. The attributes of God will be fully experienced by his people and will be reflected by his people. If it sounds like an idealized picture — everything as it should be, the land abounding in productivity — that is because it is. Truly, God comes to us in marvelous ways, here and now. But there is coming a day when things really will be as they ought to be — we can be assured of that.

We live between a period and an ellipsis. We know what has happened: Christ has come into our world and into our lives. We know what does happen: We harm our relationship with God by our sinfulness, and we need restoration. And we know what will happen: God will make his presence known among us when his Son returns, when his world is made productive as he meant it to be, and when full peace is established. Let us live between the Advents, then, with assurance — the assurance that comes from God's Word, our experiences with God, and God's promises.

Testimony

John 1:6-8, 19-28

In the rural church where my family worshiped and served during my childhood and youth, the midweek prayer service usually included a time for people to share their personal testimonies. Many people would take advantage of the opportunity. Some would go into long narratives describing the many things that the Lord had done in their lives. Some would offer simple statements of thanksgiving or requests for prayer. Standing up on a Wednesday night and saying something about what the Lord meant to you was something of a rite of passage in our church, a sort of Baptist bar mitzvah or bat mitzvah, you might say. And so it came to pass that at one of those services when I was about ten years old, I stood on trembling legs and said in a quavering voice, "I'd like to say that I love the Lord. Pray for me and my family," and I sat down. I felt relieved. I felt happy. And I felt proud. And there was the danger.

Our Testimony Is About Jesus And Not About Us

"Who are you?" they asked John. "Who are you to testify the way you do, to speak the way you do?" How tempting it could have been in such a situation to say, "Why, I'm John the Baptist, that's who I am! I'm the one 'sent from God' (v. 6)! I'm the guy who wears clothes made of camel hair and who eats locusts and wild honey (Matthew 3:4)! I'm the one who has the truth from God and who has a whole gang of people following him, which proves, of course, that I have the truth from God! That's who I am — I'm John! Remember that name — John!" The risk was the risk of recognition. John was being recognized for what he was doing. Recognition means that you are drawing attention. Often when we draw attention we want to draw more attention. Pride can rear its ugly head.

The Gospel of John emphasizes the fact that John the Baptist came, not to call attention to himself, but rather "as a witness to testify to the light.... He himself was not the light, but came to testify to the light" (vv. 7a, 8). He had come to testify to the light that had come into the world, and that light of the world was Jesus. His testimony was that he was not the Messiah (v. 20) but that he was a voice testifying to the Messiah (v. 23). It was not about him; it was about Jesus. It is not about us; it is about Jesus.

Our Testimony Emerges From Our Lives

And yet — and yet — in a way it was about John and in a way it is about us. After all, we can only testify truthfully to what we know. John could only bear witness to what he had experienced; we can only bear witness to what we have experienced. What we truly know and what we have genuinely experienced gets down deep into our lives and changes who and what we are. It will show. Therefore, John's life had to reflect his relationship with God and with God's Son, Jesus Christ; our lives have to reflect our relationship with God and with God's Son, Jesus Christ. We can only bear valid witness with our lives. We can only bear valid witness to the light of the world when our lives are reflecting his light. So there is a tension with which we live as we testify to the light that has changed our lives. The only means with which we have to witness is our lives. But the witness of our lives is to Jesus, not to ourselves. It's a tough but necessary line to walk.

John the Baptist is a positive model for us here. He said of the Messiah of whom he was testifying, "I am not worthy to untie the thong of his sandal" (v. 27). In other words, John had a servant mentality. He had a genuine sense of humility because he had a genuine grasp of who Jesus was. Perhaps the best way to bear witness to Jesus with our lives is to live servant lives — lives in which our priority is to serve God by serving others. Living a servant life is all about giving ourselves away. Such a life is a life of testimony because testimony is a giving away of self; when we testify, be it through words or through actions, something from us is being given to our world and to the people living in it. The candles that offer their light during the Advent season offer a testimony to this reality.

> *A Christmas candle is a lovely thing;*
> *It makes no noise at all,*
> *But softly gives itself away;*
> *While quite unselfish, it grows small.*[6]

We testify of Jesus with our lives when we give ourselves away. But it is the presence of the Messiah in our lives that causes and enables us to give ourselves away in ways that are appropriate as his disciples.

So here we come to the central reality of Advent, the incarnation event. John the Baptist is indeed a fine model for us, but our primary model is the Savior who was born in Bethlehem. We serve and follow the Savior

> *who, though he was in the form of God,*
> *did not regard equality with God*
> *as something to be exploited,*
> *but emptied himself,*
> *taking the form of a slave,*
> *being born in human likeness.*
> *And being found in human form,*
> *he humbled himself*
> *and became obedient to the point of death —*
> *even death on a cross.* — Philippians 2:6-8

In the incarnation event Jesus Christ became the ultimate servant. As the lives of those who are his disciples come to be caught up more and more in his life, Jesus' servant nature will become more and more our servant nature. We will testify more and more of his life and his love by the way his life and love show through us.

Our Testimony Should Lead Others
To Illumination Rather Than To Blindness

The risk is still there, though, that we will, because of pride and selfishness and weakness, come to focus more on how our testimony makes us look than on how it reflects on Jesus. If our light shines in such an inadequate way, it is damaging to us. As Harry Emerson Fosdick said, "A person completely wrapped up in himself makes a small package."[7] And as he remains wrapped up in himself the wrapping will get tighter and tighter, making him smaller and smaller. In J. R. R. Tolkien's *The Lord of the Rings*, Gollum is someone who once possessed the powerful ring. His desire to keep it and then to reclaim it caused him to change both inwardly and outwardly into a wretched, miserable character. Selfishness and grasping will inevitably cause you to shrivel up and become nothing.

If our light shines in such an inadequate way it is also damaging to others. Our testimony is meant to shed light on Jesus; testimony that focuses on self can prevent others from seeing him.

The film, *The Day of the Triffids*, is not a Christmas movie by a long shot. It is a science fiction film from the early 1960s. As the film opens, a sailor is in a London hospital, his eyes completely covered by heavy bandages because he is recovering from eye surgery. It is sometime after dark. Radio news reports herald what everyone is seeing anyway: a spectacularly beautiful meteor shower. The hospital staff members marvel with the appropriate "oohs" and "ahs" as they witness the event. Sadly, or so it seems, the sailor can see none of it. Come the next morning, however, things have changed. The sailor awakens to the day that is supposed to bring the removal of his bandages and, hopefully, the restoration of his vision. But no one comes to remove the bandages. Finally, he removes them himself, only to discover that he is the only person around who can see. Everyone who had gazed on the meteor shower is blind; he, the lone sightless one the night before, is the only one who can see!

Light is supposed to help us see. In that old sci-fi film, the light caused blindness. Here between the Advents, we Christians are to be, like John the Baptist, bearing testimony to the light of the world with our lives and with our words. Having the servant mind of Christ become more and more our mind causes us to bear ever more accurate witness about who Jesus Christ really is. We dare not let our testimony become motivated by pride and self-centeredness, because then the light we offer might result in blindness rather than illumination.

Fulfillment

Luke 1:26-38

The closer Christmas gets the more the tension builds. Can't you feel it? When Christmas Eve arrives the children will be nestled all snug in their beds, while visions of presents dance in their heads. And parents will find their sleep very hard, as they think about the charges on their credit cards. Yes, it is coming. Soon there will be no shopping days left before Christmas; then, the preliminaries will be over and the main event will arrive.

So will the anticipation of our culture be fulfilled. More importantly, however, is the fact that the anticipation of the church will be fulfilled, too. For weeks now we have observed this season of Advent, the time of preparation for the coming of Christ in the manger of Bethlehem, and the time of preparation for his future coming in power. We will continue, I suppose, to await the Second Advent, but the time for the celebration of the first one is here. We are on the edge of our seats, waiting for something to happen.

Mary was waiting for something to happen, too. She was betrothed, which means that she had entered into a legal marriage arrangement, but the relationship had not been consummated. So she was waiting for the marriage to become "official," for her life as "Mrs. Joseph" to begin. Many of you know what that is like, making all the arrangements, preparing the house, saving the money. It was an exciting time for Mary, this time of anticipation, this time of awaiting fulfillment.

Yes, Mary was waiting, she was anticipating. And something indeed happened, but it was not that for which she was waiting — it was something else altogether. Because into her everyday expectations, into her everyday hopes, into her everyday dreams, God came! And when God comes, something happens. And oh, did something happen in the life of Mary! And oh, did something happen in the life of the world!

So in the midst of her anticipation Mary experienced fulfillment from God. We can learn some things about the fulfillment of our hopes from her experience.

Fulfillment Comes Where We Are (vv. 26-30)

When Gabriel came to Mary he came to her where she was and how she was. He was a messenger from heaven who came to Mary on earth in her village of Nazareth. Mary is now in heaven enjoying God's ultimate fulfillment, but at this point in her life, she did not have to go to heaven to find fulfillment; heaven came to her. We can look forward to the great events of the future, and we should: the event of Christ's Second Coming, the event of our entry into the celestial beauties of heaven, the event of the resurrection — but we can also find great fulfillment here and now. Mary did, and we can, too, because of the event that brought her fulfillment: Christmas!

Fulfillment not only comes to us in our physical location, it also comes to us in our personal location. It comes to us where we are as people. He comes to us in his grace and in our weakness. The angel said to Mary, "You have found favor with God" (v. 30). Earlier he had called her "favored one" (v. 28). The word "favor" is the word "grace." God came to Mary just like she was. He comes to us just like we are, wherever we are.

Paul Tillich has told of some Jews who lived for a time in a grave in a Polish cemetery. There they found a place where they could escape the Nazi gas chambers. A woman gave birth to a baby in that grave, assisted by an elderly grave digger. When the baby was born, the grave digger prayed, "Great God, hast Thou finally sent the Messiah to us? For who else than the Messiah himself can be born in a grave?"[8] Commenting on that story, Welton Gaddy said, "Well, that child was not the Messiah, but an important point about the Messiah had been made. Christ comes to us in the depths — at our worst times, in our weakest moments. Christ is born."[9]

Yes, Christ comes to us in the depths, if that is where we are. He comes to us in the heights, if that is where we are. No matter where we are, there he comes. His coming is an act of grace.

Fulfillment Comes In The Promises Of God (vv. 31-33)

When the angel came to Mary, he came to tell her something, and when he spoke to her, he spoke the language of promise. The words he spoke to Mary stand in the tradition of Old Testament messianic prophecies.[10] For centuries the Hebrew people had received promises from God that one day a Messiah would come and would deliver God's people from all their oppression. There was no expectation, however, that the fulfillment would come in the person of a baby born in a stable and placed in a manger.

But before the baby came there came more words. There came more promises. "You will conceive in your womb and bear a son." "He will be great, and will be called the Son of the Most High." "The Lord God will give to him the throne of his ancestor David. He will reign over the house of Jacob forever, and of his kingdom there will be no end." Words. Promises.

We might not blame the Hebrews for feeling like the continually put-off lover who has had the same conversation with her intended too many times.

"You said we were going to get married."

"We are."

"When?"

"Soon."

"How soon?"

"Real soon."

And the woman thinks to herself, "Words. Promises. Again." Finally she says, "Let's set the date and see the ring." It is hard to find marital fulfillment in words and promises. Too often a suitor's actions do not match his words.

The angel came to Mary with words and with promises. Now, in her case, the thing shortly came to pass. Such, however, is not always the case. We have made progress as Christians when we find fulfillment in the promises and words of God and do not insist on seeing the "proof."

We need to be reminded that the Word of God is an active thing. Old Testament messianic prophecies were not just words; they were the beginning of a process that was sure to be completed.

As Sidney Greidanus has reminded us, the Hebrew term often translated "word" (*dabar*) also means "deed." He comments, "Whenever the prophets faithfully proclaimed the word of God ... that word was not merely something 'which was said,' information about God's will for the present or his plan for the future, but that word was a deed of God, setting in motion the content of the message."[11]

Can we come to see fulfillment in the Word of God? Will we believe his promises to us? Will we believe that his Son really come to us in our lives? God has said that he will — so he will! It is set in motion; it will happen.

Fulfillment Comes When We Believe (vv. 34-38)

Mary's final statement in this exchange with the angel was, "Here am I, the servant of the Lord; let it be with me according to your word" (v. 38). Fulfillment comes when we believe, for believing leads to submission to the will of God. For the believer, fulfillment in this life is finally found in submission to God and to his will.

Lest we think that Mary slid easily into this belief and fulfillment, let us notice that Mary had questions and concerns, problems and hesitations. The greeting of the angel had troubled her (v. 29). She heard the word that she would have a son but she pointed out that she, at that point, had no husband (v. 34). A good, solid question, that one! You see, doubts and questions are allowed, even for God's faithful ones, but they should be stepping stones on the path to submission.

There is a certain co-dependency in such discipleship. God allowed Mary to learn from, and to be inspired by, the life of her kinswoman Elizabeth. As reassurance to Mary that this remarkable thing would indeed happen, Gabriel told her of Elizabeth's pregnancy (v. 36). Similarly, we can be taught and inspired by the experiences of God's fulfillment that other believers have, and, when we experience his fulfillment, we can share the experience with others. We need each other as we submit ourselves to God.

Still, when all was said and done, Mary chose simply to believe and simply to submit. In a Christmas sermon, Walter Brueggemann said, "Bet on the baby."[12] Mary bet on the Word of God concerning the baby, and the baby came. He fulfilled the promises and purposes of God. Will you "bet on the baby?" Will you believe the promises of the Lord and, with eyes of faith, see that his Word is taking place through the baby?

To live between the Advents is to live between two events of fulfillment. Jesus came in Bethlehem, thus fulfilling the prophecies about the coming Messiah. Jesus will come in power, thus fulfilling the prophecies about his Second Advent. In between, we find fulfillment where we are by believing God's Word and submitting ourselves to his will. Such fulfillment requires that we "bet on the baby." Will you?

Endnotes

1. *Preaching* (November/December, 1990), p. 41.

2. William L. Lane, *The Gospel of Mark* (Grand Rapids: Eerdmans, 1974), pp. 444-448.

3. *Ibid.*, p. 448.

4. Mark Galli, "In Praise of Foolish Lovers," *Christianity Today* (November 19, 1990), pp. 35-36.

5. *Preaching* (November/December, 1990), p. 41.

6. Eva K. Logue, cited in Frank S. Mead, editor & compiler, *The Encyclopedia of Religious Quotations* (Old Tappan: Spire, 1976), p. 111.

7. Harry Emerson Fosdick, *On Being a Real Person* (New York: Harper & Brothers, 1943), pp. 83-84.

8. Paul Tillich, *The Shaking of the Foundations* (New York: Charles Scribner's Sons, 1948), p. 165, cited in C. Welton Gaddy, *Tuning the Heart: University Sermons* (Macon: Mercer University, 1990), p. 148.

9. *Op. cit.*, Gaddy.

10. Gail R. O'Day, *Pulpit Digest* (November/December, 1990), p. 89: "The Gospel Lesson shows how the Messianic hope of 2 Samuel 7 was carried forward into the New Testament. The language of verses 32 and 33 is particularly important in this regard, because it is a deliberate echo of 2 Samuel 7:12-16."

11. Sidney Greidanus, *The Modern Preacher and the Ancient Text: Interpreting and Preaching Biblical Literature* (Grand Rapids: Eerdmans, 1988), p. 3.

12. Walter Brueggemann, "A Time Bomb Among the Superpowers," *Pulpit Digest* (November/December, 1990), p. 17.

Part Two

While We Wait

Watching And Working

Mark 13:24-37

Our focus during the season of Advent is on the arrival of Jesus Christ. There are three ways to think about that arrival. First, we may reflect upon the arrival of Jesus Christ in the incarnation event. Our attention is on the manger of Bethlehem and the inbreaking of God into our world there. Second, we may reflect upon the arrival of Jesus Christ in our own personal lives. We give attention to what Jesus has already done in our lives, and we remain open to the new things Jesus may do in our lives as he comes to us today. Third, we may reflect upon the arrival of Jesus Christ when he comes again. We focus on the Second Coming of Jesus and we think about ways in which we should be ready for that Advent.

Someone has said that Advent is the "Season of Surprise."[1] That is an excellent way to think of this Advent season. Jesus came in surprising ways when he was born in Bethlehem. One of the reasons that so many people in his day missed his coming or failed to grasp its significance is that he came in an unexpected manner. One of the reasons we should be very careful in our thinking about the Second Coming is that God has a tendency to do things in surprising ways. Let's not think we have it all figured out! Many of the folks in the first century thought they had it all figured out, and they missed it! More to the point for today, though, is the fact that the Lord may be ready to come to us in surprising ways during this Advent season. Let's be open to his coming!

Watching

In Mark 13, Jesus is answering a question posed to him by some of his disciples. The question was prompted by their visit to the Jerusalem temple just before the arrest and crucifixion of Christ. The disciples were impressed by the magnificence of the temple

(v. 1). Jesus responded to their expressions of awe by predicting the destruction of the temple (v. 2). After Jesus and the disciples had left the temple and gone to the Mount of Olives, four of the disciples asked Jesus, "Tell us, when will this be, and what will be the sign that all these things are about to be accomplished?" (v. 4).

Watch Events, But Don't Be Fooled By Events

In response, Jesus began to tell the disciples of things for which to watch. Now, we need to know this truth: from the perspective of the disciples of Jesus, the fulfillment of Jesus' words about the destruction of the temple and the things leading up to it occurred within thirty years' time. It was during the Jewish rebellion against Rome in 66-70 C.E. that such atrocities occurred and the temple was burned and razed. As the disciples prepared for that occurrence, look at the kinds of things that Jesus told them to watch out for.

"*Beware that no one leads you astray*" (vv. 5, 22-23). Look very carefully at that for which Jesus tells his followers to look.

> *Many will come in my name and say, "I am he!" and they will lead many astray. When you hear of wars and rumors of wars, do not be alarmed; this must take place, but the end is still to come. For nation will rise against nation, and kingdom against kingdom; there will be earthquakes in various places; there will be famines. This is but the beginning of the birthpangs.*
> — Mark 13:6-8

> *And if any one says to you at that time, "Look! Here is the Messiah!" or "Look! There he is!"* — *do not believe it. False messiahs and false prophets will appear and produce signs and omens, to lead astray, if possible, the elect.*   — Mark 13:21-22

That's what Jesus told the disciples to look out for in relation to the coming event, in their own lifetime, of the destruction of the temple. "Pay attention to what's going on," he said, "but don't make too much of it. Don't try to turn something into a sign of the end that is not in fact a sign of the end."

"As for yourselves, beware" (v. 9). Jesus reminded his disciples that in the difficult days leading up to the destruction of the temple they would endure suffering, persecution, and tribulation. Their calling was to endure by relying on the Holy Spirit rather than on their own strength and wisdom. Such is our calling, too.

The instruction to take heed is for us, also. Throughout the last 2,000 years of history, wars and rumors of wars have taken place. Earthquakes and other natural disasters have occurred. False prophets and messianic pretenders have proliferated. Such things are but the beginning of the birthpangs. We do well to pay attention, but we also do well not to make more of events than we should. In the meantime, we rely on God's presence with us through his Holy Spirit. Only as we rely on him can we persevere. Make no mistake about it, the time will come when some generation, and it may be ours, "will see the Son of man coming in clouds with great power and glory." Until then, we trust and persevere.

Working

Is it enough to just wait and watch for Christ to come? That depends on how active our waiting and watching are.

The hymn that begins "O land of rest, for thee I sigh" has an interesting and uncertain history. It did not always have a refrain. The earlier version of the refrain, though, was "We'll *wait* till Jesus comes." Only later, under revivalistic influence, was the refrain changed to "We'll *work* till Jesus comes."[2] Both emphases seem to me to be important. We certainly are waiting for Jesus to come. But while we are waiting, we are to be working.

Jesus said that we should be watching because his return could be at any time. He used the parable of the man going on a journey to make his point. Like the servants of the man, we don't want to be found sleeping. We want always to be watching and waiting. But I am struck by a particular phrase in the parable: "It is like a man going on a journey, when he leaves home and puts his servants in charge, *each with his work* ..." (v. 34). We each have our work to do while we live in these days and while we await the

Second Advent of our Lord. We do that in light of the First Advent and in light of the ongoing presence of Christ with us.

The story is told of an eclipse in colonial New England during which state legislators panicked and several moved to adjourn. But one of them said, "Mr. Speaker, if it is not the end of the world and we adjourn, we shall appear to be fools. If it is the end of the world, I should choose to be found doing my duty. I move you, Sir, that candles be brought."[3]

Indeed, when the end comes, we would choose to be found doing our duty. If the end does not come soon, we would still choose to be found doing our duty. No matter what, then, we are to be doing our duty, to be carrying out our work. I would say two things about our work as we wait:

We work in God's power. As we do our work, we do well to remember the words of Paul to the church at Corinth: "You are not lacking in any spiritual gift as you wait for the revealing of our Lord Jesus Christ" (1 Corinthians 1:7). We wait and we work as empowered, gifted Christians. We are to be careful, as Paul warned the Corinthian Christians at later points, not to think more of our gifts than we ought. Whatever gifts and abilities God has given us he has given us out of his grace and not because of our merit. He has given them for his purposes and not for our glorification. Nevertheless, let us rely on God's power with us, on the gifts he has given us, rather than on our own strength and power. The work is finally his work, and he will empower us to do it.

We work in Jesus' spirit. The work we have to do is Jesus' work. We are his disciples. We are his followers. We are his people. As the body of Christ we have the responsibility every single day to continue his mission and ministry. What is that mission and ministry? We could put it in many ways. "To be vehicles for the inbreaking of the kingdom of God." "To bear witness to the love of God." "To preach the gospel to the lost." "To be witnesses to our community and to the world." All those and other phrases would summarize our task well.

It comes down to this. The incarnation, the coming of Christ all those years ago, means that God came and dwelt with us. God was in Christ, reconciling the world unto himself. In a different way, but nonetheless in a real way, the church as the body of Christ continues to show the world the love and the ways of God. We are to do that like Jesus did it, if we are to do it at all. How do we do it like he did it? By breaking into people's lives, by being bold in our witness, and by being up front about who the Lord is to us. But we do that in humility. We do it in love. We do it in grace. We do it with gentleness. We do it with sacrifice. At least, if we do it like Jesus did it, that's how we do it.

In a *Peanuts* comic strip, Lucy was telling Linus what a good evangelist she would be. "I could be a terrific evangelist. Do you know that kid who sits behind me in school? I convinced him that my religion is better than his religion." Linus asked, "How did you do that?" Lucy replied, "I hit him with my lunch box." And then there is this epitaph written by C. S. Lewis:

> *This stone erected by her sorrowing brothers*
> *In memory of Martha Clay.*
> *Here lies one who lived for others,*
> *Now she has peace. And so have they!*[4]

We'll work till Jesus comes, all right, but we'll work till Jesus comes like Jesus himself worked. We'll work in faith, in obedience, in openness, with vulnerability, and in utter humility, always putting the other before ourselves, and not trying to grasp more for ourselves than we should. We'll work in love, because that's how Jesus worked!

Conclusion

Mark 13 is a very confusing chapter to many students of the Bible, and the source of that confusion seems to be that Jesus talks with his disciples about two different but related things: that which would happen in their own lifetimes and that which would happen as some indeterminate date. Jesus would say the same kinds of things to us today, I believe. He would want us to pay attention to, and to be mindful of, those things that are happening in our own time, but not to make more of them than we should. At the same time, he would want us to have no doubt that sometime, maybe sooner, maybe later, he will come again in power. And, he would want us, in any time, to watch, wait, and to work. He would want us to work like he did, trusting in the Father, being obedient to the Father, depending on the power of God, and living sacrificial, loving lives.

Taking Advantage Of The Opportunity
Mark 1:1-8; 2 Peter 3:8-15a

Different people have differing perspectives on time. At no time of year is that more evident than at this one. Our little ones think that Christmas will never arrive. The rest of us think that last Christmas just happened a couple of months ago.

Differing perspectives on time are not restricted to the holiday season, though. I learned recently of an organization called the Long Now Foundation. The foundation encourages us to think with a much longer-term perspective than we usually do. According to their information:

> It has been nearly 10,000 years since the end of the last ice age and the emergence of modern civilization. Progress during that time was often measured on a "faster/cheaper" scale. The Long Now Foundation seeks to promote "slower/better" thinking and to focus our collective creativity on the next 10,000 years.

The roots of the foundation lie in the idea of a computer scientist named Daniel Hillis. In 1993, he wrote:

> When I was a child, people used to talk about what would happen by the year 2000. Now, thirty years later, they still talk about what will happen by the year 2000. The future has been shrinking by one year per year for my entire life. I think it is time for us to start a long-term project that gets people thinking past the mental barrier of the millennium. I would like to propose a large ... mechanical clock, powered by seasonal temperature changes. It ticks once a year, bongs once a century, and the cuckoo comes out every millennium.[5]

I will avoid the obvious joke about the cuckoos that come out every millennium. What did catch my attention was the way in which this group takes a long-term view of history. They are actually symbolizing their view by constructing just such a millennial clock. "This world has a long time ahead of it," they seem to be saying. "Let's take a long-term view and get ready for the next ten thousand years."

Contrast with the viewpoint of the Long Now Foundation that of the *Bulletin of the Atomic Scientists*, a viewpoint symbolized by another, decidedly different kind of clock. Since 1947, the cover of the *Bulletin* has featured the Doomsday Clock. This clock symbolizes how close, in the estimation of atomic scientists, our world is to a nuclear catastrophe. With midnight standing for the time such a catastrophe would take place, the clock has for the last fifty years stood somewhere between seventeen and three minutes to midnight. The first clock stood at seven minutes to midnight. The closest to midnight it was ever moved was in 1953, just after both the United States and the Soviet Union conducted successful hydrogen bomb tests. The scientists set the clock at two minutes to midnight. As recently as 1984, during an intensifying arms race, the clock was set at three minutes to midnight. The last time the clock was adjusted was in 2002, when it was set at seven minutes to midnight.[6]

Do you see the difference in the two perspectives? One perspective says, "We have thousands of years of history left, so let's take full advantage of the opportunity." The other perspective says, "We may have little time left, so let's do something about it." Either perspective, when taken seriously, should spur us on to action.

Peter offered his original readers and us a perspective that is a combination of the long-term and the short-term view. On the one hand he said, "With the Lord one day is like a thousand years" (3:8). On the other hand he said, "The day of the Lord will come like a thief" (3:10), that is, suddenly and unexpectedly. In light of both realities, Peter said, there is incentive to act. There is tremendous opportunity in these days, just as there was tremendous opportunity in Peter's day. We have the opportunity to repent and the opportunity to grow.

The Opportunity To Repent

We are inclined to misinterpret delay. If something needs to be done and a person takes a long while to do it, we interpret that as procrastination or as laziness, and that may be. On the other hand, it may be that the person has a very good reason for the delay. Planning may need to be done. Further maturity may be in order for the group or person to be targeted by the action. Or, if some judgment needs to be passed or some punishment needs to be inflicted and the person responsible for meting out the judgment does not do so quickly, we might interpret that delay as weakness. The fact may be that an opportunity for change is being provided.

Already in the first century, people were wondering what was taking God so long to send Jesus back. Scoffers were saying that the world had been around for a long time and would certainly continue; there was no evidence that it would come to an end. Peter responded that the Lord had destroyed the world once by water and would do so again by fire (vv. 3-7).

Moreover, Peter reminded his readers that the Lord's time frame is not our time frame. A thousand years and a day, a day and 1,000 years — it's all the same to God. We are bound by and to the clock and the calendar; God is not. Therefore, to try to restrict God to our view of time, to our notion of what is a long time or a short time, is to try to limit God, and that is always inappropriate.

Most importantly, the delay by God in sending Jesus is not a sign of slowness or inability or inattention. No, the delay by God is a matter of grace. It is a matter of forbearance. It is a matter of patience. "The Lord is not slow about his promise, as some think of slowness, but is patient with you, not wanting any to perish, but all to come to repentance" (v. 9). The time that the Lord has granted to our world has stretched on for another 2,000 years. The time that the Lord has given you has stretched on now for however long your life has been. If you have not accepted him as your Savior, you still have the opportunity to repent.

Sometimes we have to live a long time and go through a lot before we are in a position truly to understand and accept God's grace. Perhaps the world has to get to a very low point before some of us will ever see the need to repent. Or, maybe your personal life has to deteriorate to a certain point before you will see the need to repent. It certainly does not have to be that way, but even if things get worse as time goes by, the time that goes by is a sign of God's grace and patience. Philip Yancey tells this story:

> *When Bill Moyers filmed a television special on the hymn "Amazing Grace," his camera followed Johnny Cash into the bowels of a maximum-security prison. "What does this song mean to you?" Cash asked the prisoners after singing the hymn. One man serving time for attempted murder replied, "I'd been a deacon, a churchman, but I never knew what grace was until I ended up in a place like this."*[7]

"I never knew what grace was until I ended up in a place like this." What kind of place are you in? Are you finally in the place where you are ready to know what grace is? Are you in a place where you are finally ready to repent?

Some of the scariest words I ever hear people say are "I'll get my life right with God when I'm ready." Yes, God is patient. God is forbearing, but time is not unlimited. Remember, the same God for whom 1,000 years is as a day is also the God whose Son will come like a thief in the night. You have the opportunity the repent *now*. What will you do with it? As the hymn challenges us:

> *While we pray and while we plead, While you see your soul's deep need,*
> *While our Father calls you home, Will you not, my brother, come?*
> *You have wandered far away; Do not risk another day;*
> *Do not turn from God your face, But today accept His grace.*
> *Why not now? Why not now? Why not come to Jesus now?*
> *Why not now? Why not now? Why not come to Jesus now?*[8]

Now is the time of salvation for you. Why not come to him now? John the Baptist challenged his listeners to get ready for the coming of the Messiah by repenting of their sins. The challenge is the same for us, except that we repent because the Messiah has come and because he is coming again.

The Opportunity To Grow

Once you repent there is still a long way to go. Many of us repented and became Christians, long ago or recently. Whether you have been a Christian for decades or whether you become a Christian today, you still have a lot of growing to do. When we trust Jesus as Savior we also acknowledge him as Lord of our lives. His lingering, his delay in returning, gives all of us a tremendous opportunity to grow in our relationship with him. When he comes, don't we want him to find us to be people who have grown and matured in ways that will please him?

Peter reminds us that we are to be becoming disciples who live "lives of holiness and godliness" (v. 11), so that we will "be found by him at peace, without spot or blemish" (v. 14). What does it mean to be holy and godly, without spot or blemish? There is a moral connotation here. Our lives are being molded by God to be more and more like Jesus. We are not to let the world dictate what kinds of lives we live. Cleansed by the blood of Jesus and empowered by the Spirit of God, we are being shaped into people who bear witness with our lives to who God is. We are not saved by works; we are saved only by the grace of God that we experience through faith. We are not doomed or even crippled in our discipleship when we sin after we are saved. But, the fact is that if you have a real encounter with the living God through his crucified and resurrected Son, Jesus Christ, you will be changed. Some of that change will be instantaneous. Much of that change will happen over a long period of time, but where God works change takes place, and it is change for the better. We want to use what time we have left bearing witness to Christ with our lives and doing things that build up rather than tear down. Morality does matter.

But being holy and godly without spot or blemish is not just about morals; it is also about service. This kind of language is typically used in the Bible to describe people and things that are set aside for use in service to God. As we grow in our relationship with God, we realize that while we are saved from our sin, we are also saved to serve. When our Christian faith really takes hold of us, when we are seized by the reality of all that Christ has done for us, we become people who give of ourselves in service to God. How do we serve God? By serving others. Is there lots of time left before Christ returns? If so, that is good — it gives us lots of time to grow in service. Is there only a little time left? If so, that is good — it gives us incentive to do all that we can while we have the opportunity.

Conclusion

We are Christians, followers of Jesus Christ. That makes us people with a long-term perspective who are ready for whatever happens in the short term. We assume that we have 10,000 years to work and to serve and we are always looking forward. Yet we know that Christ could return in the next second and we want to be found fulfilling our calling. Either way, now is the only time we have. Now is the time to take advantage of the opportunity. If you don't know Christ as your Savior, now is the time to take advantage of the opportunity to repent. If you are a Christian but you have not been taking full advantage of the time that has been given to you, now is the time to take advantage of the opportunity to commit yourself to fuller service.

On Being Safe And Sound

1 Thessalonians 5:16-24

The season is all about being ready when somebody comes. Many of us will be getting ready for family members to come at Christmas. Our young ones are trying to clean up their lives (and maybe even their rooms) so that they will be ready for old Saint Nick.

Yes, we are getting ready for folks to come. Above all others, though, we are getting ready for Jesus to come. It is almost too obvious even to point out that Jesus has already come, all those years ago in Bethlehem. It is also obvious that he has come many times since, as he has come to live in our hearts and lives and to be with us day by day as Savior and Lord. We are also aware that Jesus can and will come to us in our own lives right here and right now in new and challenging ways. The focus of our text, though, is on being ready for the Second Coming of Christ. Perhaps we should all remember that the ways in which we need to prepare for the Second Coming of Christ are also the ways in which we need to prepare for the new and challenging comings of Christ into our lives in the here and now.

We want to be ready for Christ to come. When he returns, we want to be ready to meet him. That desire to be ready can intimidate us. After all, we are deeply aware of our sins. We are deeply aware of our imperfections. We are deeply aware of our failings. We are deeply aware of our prejudices, of our bigotries, of our jealousies, and of our fears. We feel incapable of becoming the kind of people who are truly and fully ready for Jesus to come. We know that when we try to pull ourselves up by our own bootstraps our hands tend to slip. We know that sometimes our best efforts to climb out of a hole just land us deeper in the hole, like in those old movies in which someone tries and tries to get out of a pit but just keeps sliding down the wall. Here is the burning question: If it is beyond our capabilities to be ready, how can we possibly be ready? We want to be safely in the arms of God when Jesus comes, but to be safe we must be sound. That is, we must be people of wholeness and integrity in our relationship with God. How can that be if we are so incapable?

The answer to the question lies in the form of our passage and in a word contained in our passage. Notice that the passage is formed as a prayer: "May the God of peace himself ..." (v. 23). We can be ready for the coming of Jesus only as we are made ready by God himself. Trying to make yourself ready, trying to be good enough, trying to be holy enough, can only lead to two conclusions: either an utter sense of failure or a false sense of pride. Neither conclusion is worthy of a disciple. Only God can work in your life to make you what you ought to be so you have to be open to the work of God in your life. He is called here the "God of peace," which means that he is the God who causes peace and who gives us peace. That peace is wholeness of relationship with God, with ourselves, and with others. Only God can do what needs to be done to bring about peace.

I said that the answer to the question, "How can we possibly be ready when Jesus comes?" lies in the form of the passage and in a word in the passage. That word is "sanctification," a good old word that has been neglected in many Christian circles. "To sanctify" means "to make holy." "To make holy" means to set apart from the common or the profane. It means to be pure in the sense that you are ready for service. Again, only God can do this. Only God can sanctify or make holy because only God is sanctified or holy. We can be sanctified because of what God has done in Christ. Only in relationship with God can we be made holy.

I wonder what such a holy, sanctified (maybe better put "becoming sanctified"), ready for Jesus to come person would look like? I wonder what such a person would be like. With full awareness that we should resist the temptation to attempt to fit people into a "one-size-fits-all" box, I offer two examples from the Bible and one from fiction.

The two biblical examples are drawn from the Gospel of Luke. Luke, alone among the gospel writers, tells us of these two people. I point us to them because they are identified as people who were so ready for the First Coming of Jesus that they immediately recognized him even when he was only about forty days old.

The first is Simeon, who, upon seeing the baby Jesus, said, "Master, now you are dismissing your servant in peace, according to your word; for my eyes have seen your salvation, which you have prepared in the presence of all peoples ..." (Luke 2:29-31). The vast majority of people in the first century were not ready to recognize Jesus as Messiah when he was an adult. Why was this man so ready to recognize him when he was just a baby? For one thing, he was "looking forward to the consolation of Israel ..." (v. 25), which means that he was looking for the Messiah to come. For another thing, and this one is crucial for us, "the Holy Spirit rested on him" (v. 25). Indeed, he was in the temple on that crucial day because the Spirit had led him there (v. 27). Here was a man who was being worked on by the Holy Spirit. Here was a man who was being led by the Holy Spirit. Here was someone who was ready for the coming of Jesus because he had been growing and learning and maturing, all under the influence of the Holy Spirit. So, I conclude from that truth that one way in which the Lord will make us ready, whole, and mature is through the activity of the Holy Spirit. Are you open to what the Spirit wants to teach you?

Then there is Anna, the 84-year-old prophetess. A widow for most of her life, we are told that when she saw the baby Jesus "she began to praise God and to speak about the child to all who were looking for the redemption of Jerusalem" (Luke 2:38). What gave her such insight? We are told that "she never left the temple but worshiped there with fasting and prayer night and day" (v. 37). Again, this is not about what she was able to do for herself. It is rather about what she was open to God doing through her. God had easy access to her life because she intentionally made herself available to him, and God had her ready because of her continual worshiping, fasting, and praying. The spiritual disciplines are important, you see, as avenues through which God prepares us, changes us, and matures us. We need to be in worship and we need to be constantly in conversation with God. Are you putting yourself in a position to be open to God?

The example I offer from fiction is the character Artaban in Henry van Dyke's little book, *The Story of the Other Wise Man*.[9] Artaban was to join the other three Wise Men on their trek to Israel to see the new king whose birth the strange star signified. He had sold his house and all his possessions in order to acquire his gift for the child, a gift comprised of three jewels: a sapphire, a ruby, and a pearl. The agreement he had with his friends was that when the star they had seen appeared again, he would meet them where they were and they would journey together to Israel. He was ten days' journey from his three friends and they made it clear that they would wait no longer than ten days. Sure enough, the star appeared and Artaban set out. On the tenth day of his journey, when he was just a few hours from the rendezvous point, he came across an injured man. What should he do? His conscience told him to help the man, but his schedule told him to press on. His conscience won out and he stopped to aid the injured man. As it happened, the man was a Hebrew who told Artaban that the great king of the Jews was to be born in Bethlehem, not Jerusalem. Artaban left and reached the place of meeting, but his friends had already left. Artaban had to sell the sapphire to acquire provisions for his own journey to Bethlehem.

When he arrived in Bethlehem, he found no sign of the family he was seeking. He did chance upon a house where a young mother was caring for her small son. She told him that a family such as he sought had been in Bethlehem and that they had attracted much attention. But immediately after being visited by three men much like Artaban, the family had left. She heard that they had gone to Egypt. Disappointed, Artaban prepared to leave, but was stopped by the sound of screaming and crying from the streets of Bethlehem. "They're killing the children," came the cries. Artaban stood in the doorway of the house as it was approached by a soldier wielding a blood-stained sword. Artaban reached into the folds of his robe and took out the ruby. He said that the ruby was for a soldier who understood that there was no one else in the house. The soldier took the ruby and went away.

Artaban then traveled to Egypt in search of the newborn king. There he met a rabbi who told him that the king of the Jews would not be found in the halls of power but with the poor, the needy, and the afflicted. Artaban journeyed all over Egypt and the rest of the Middle East, looking everywhere among the unfortunate and destitute for the king. He never found him. For 33 years he looked, and everywhere he went he helped the poor and sick and needy in every way he could.

An old man then, Artaban traveled one more time to Jerusalem. It was Passover. Hordes of people were moving together in the same direction. Someone told him that a person who some called the king of the Jews was about to be executed. Just then, a young woman who was being sold to satisfy her father's debts broke free from some soldiers who were holding her and threw herself at his feet. Artaban used his last jewel, the pearl, to ransom her. Just then a tremendous earthquake struck and a piece of tile fell from a building, striking Artaban in the head. The ransomed girl held the head of the seriously wounded wise man. She heard something that sounded musical but almost like a voice. Artaban spoke:

> *Not so, my Lord: For when saw I thee hungered and fed thee? Or thirsty, and gave thee drink? When saw I thee a stranger, and took thee in? Or naked, and clothed thee? When saw I thee sick or in prison, and came unto thee? Three-and-thirty years have I looked for thee; but I have never seen thy face, nor ministered to thee, my king.*

Then she heard the voice again, only this time the words came through: "Verily I say unto thee, inasmuch as thou hast done it unto one of the least of these my brethren, thou hast done it unto me." And Artaban died, having found the king.

Somehow, Artaban was empowered and led by God to be used as a servant, to help those who needed help, to comfort those who needed comforting. He sought no credit, for he didn't even know he was serving his king. To be sanctified like Artaban is to serve with no thought of reward but only with the desire to serve.

You see, we want to be ready when Jesus comes. We want to be ready to meet the king. To be ready, we have to be sanctified —

to be made into holy vessels of service. Only God can do that. Only God can make us safe because only God can make us sound. As the old hymn says:

> *His power can make you what you ought to be;*
> *His blood can cleanse your heart and make you free;*
> *His love can fill your soul, and you will see*
> *'Twas best for him to have his way with thee.*[10]

And when you begin thinking about being ready, remember what Paul said: "The one who calls you is faithful, and he will do this" (1 Thessalonians 5:24).

Trusting God's Promises

2 Samuel 7:1-11, 16; Luke 1:26-38

Unfortunately, in our culture we have been conditioned to expect people to break their promises. Politicians promise us all sorts of things when they are running for office, and even as we base our vote on what they say, we fully expect them to break their promises. Advertisers promise amazing results if we will just use this product or the best deal ever if we will just shop at that store, and even as we spend our money we fully expect the promise not to hold true. People promise us all sorts of things, but we are never completely surprised when they let us down. I'm afraid we have become a very cynical culture. It is hard really to disappoint us, because a big part of us expects to be disappointed.

Let us not transfer that cynicism to our thinking about God. We can expect God to fulfill his promises. The birth of Jesus Christ is a confirmation of the commitment of God to his promises. It is also an indicator of the ways in which God fulfills his promises.

One thousand years before Jesus was born, David became king of Israel. He came to that position through much turmoil and controversy, but the Old Testament affirms that he came to that position ultimately through the guiding hand of God. God loved David, and God had great plans for David and for his descendants. It occurred to David one day that it seemed wrong that he had a fine house to live in while God's presence as symbolized by the Ark of the Covenant had only a tent in which to dwell. So, David proposed the construction of a temple to the Prophet Nathan. Nathan initially approved the plan, but then was told by God to have David scrap the proposed construction. Then, God told Nathan to say two very important things to David:

> *Moreover the Lord declares to you that the Lord will make you a house.*   — 2 Samuel 7:11b

> *Your house and your kingdom shall be made sure forever before me; your throne shall be established forever.*
> — 2 Samuel 7:16

The idea was that David and his descendants would rule in Israel forever.

And rule they did, for a very long time. Through a division of the kingdom, through military coups, through moral failures, through wars, through the political and military maneuverings of the surrounding empires, the kingdom of David endured. For over 400 years a descendant of David ruled in Jerusalem. But on that dark day, in 587 B.C.E., when Nebuchadnezzar and the Babylonians destroyed Jerusalem, they also exiled King Zedekiah to Babylon. Thus ended the line of Davidic kings in Israel. Never again did a descendant of David rule in Jerusalem. Hopes persisted for a while that one would, of course. But it never happened.

At some point, Hebrew theologians began to understand the larger importance of the promise that had been made to David. One day, they began to understand, God would send the greatest descendant of David who had ever lived. He would be the ideal ruler. He would establish not only the kingdom of David but also the kingdom of God, and it would be established forever. So they waited. And waited. Some thought that God would never keep his promise. Others waited and looked; those who never stopped believing.

Cut to Nazareth, an inconspicuous village in Israel. It had been almost 600 years since the last descendant of David ruled in Jerusalem. The Angel Gabriel appeared to a young woman, probably just a teenager, named Mary. He told her that she had found favor with God and that she would conceive and bear a son whom she was to name Jesus. In telling Mary about these wonderful things, Gabriel used terms that the Jews were accustomed to hearing in describing royal figures. Among the truths that were made clear by Gabriel were that the baby would be the Son of God and that he would inherit the throne of David. His reign would last forever. In other words, in the birth of Jesus the promises made to David had been kept.

We may be sure that God will keep his promises. But we need to learn from the birth of Jesus some lessons about the ways in which he keeps those promises.

God Keeps His Promises In His Time

The logical and literal interpretation of God's promise to David would be that the line of kings descended from David would never end, that there would always be a Davidic king sitting on the Jerusalem throne. That did not happen. But in God's plan and in God's time something much greater than that happened. The Jews looked for almost 600 years for the great Messiah who would be descended from David. He finally came, but much waiting had to be done. God's time is not the same as our time. We must learn to wait on God, and in that time of waiting learn patience, endurance, and faith.

God Keeps His Promises In His Way

Seldom does God work in ways that we would expect. Seldom does God choose the people we would choose for him. God sent the angel to Mary, a virgin who was only betrothed, not yet fully married. She was poor and humble. Surely we would expect the Messiah to be born to someone whose piety was known far and wide or to someone who could give the king all the comforts and advantages one would anticipate royalty having. But that's not the way God works. That's not the way he worked when he chose Jesus' ancestor David. David was the runt of the litter, so insignificant that Jesse did not even bother to bring him in to meet Samuel until he was told to do so. But God chose David. God chose Mary out of his grace, but also because she had a humble, accepting, open heart. Perhaps we can only perceive the fulfillment of God's promises when we live in expectation that God will act, not because he owes it to us and we live lives of quiet, unassuming dependence on God.

Note one other thing about the way in which God keeps his promises. He keeps his promises in a way that provokes response and commitment. Mary asked questions. How could she not ask questions? But in the end Mary said, "Here am I, the servant of the Lord; let it be with me according to your word" (Luke 1:38). When God comes to us he comes ready to keep his promises and to work in our lives, but he does look for receptivity. He does look for response. He does look for commitment. He does look for willingness. Because you see, often the keeping of his promise to us is only the beginning of what God wants to do with us and through us. This was not the end for Mary in her walk with God. This was only the beginning. Better put, this was only the next step, but what a significant step it was! We want God to come to us, don't we? We want God to keep his promises to us, don't we? We want God to reveal himself, don't we? I don't know. Do we? Real, legitimate expectation of God's action carries with it a real, legitimate commitment to do whatever God calls us to do. God always keeps his promises to us. Do we always keep ours to him?

With these principles in our minds I would remind you that God still keeps his promises. Just as surely as he kept his promise to give David a kingdom that would last forever by sending Jesus to reign as the resurrected Lord, he will also keep his other promises. We may wait with that assurance. Here are a few of the promises we have from God that he will surely keep. I include here promises made by Jesus, the Son of God, who was fully human and fully divine.

He Will Never Leave Us Or Forsake Us

"Remember, I am with you always," Jesus said. He promised that when he ascended to the Father the Holy Spirit would come. And come the Holy Spirit did. Thus we are comforted, which is one role of the Holy Spirit. We do not suffer alone. We do not experience trials alone. We have the Comforter. Also, we are empowered. The Holy Spirit gives us gifts and empowerment to do the work of the Lord in our world. We are incapable, but God is fully capable. He is with us, giving us help and strength.

We Really Can Live As Citizens Of The Kingdom
Jesus said, "You are the light of the world." He said, "You are the salt of the earth." He said, "You will be my witnesses." We look at ourselves and say, "Who, me?" and the Lord says, "Yes, you!" We don't feel very much like salt and light and witnesses sometimes, and frankly, we don't look very much like that sometimes. The truth is, though, that when God's grace breaks into our lives it continues to work in those lives. The truth is that when we commit ourselves to following Jesus, we do become citizens of his kingdom and he gives us the strength and ability to be becoming ever more faithful and effective citizens of the kingdom.

Jesus Really Is Coming Back
God promised that he would. Here we learn valuable lessons from the First Coming of Christ. Remember that he came in God's own time. Remember that he came in God's own way. Remember that it was the meek and lowly and humble and expectant who were ready for him to come. Remember that 2,000 years in God's scheme of things is not a very long time at all. Remember to be ready.

Conclusion

God does act. God does keep his promises. God does so in his own way and in his own time, but he is faithful and sure. Still, when God acts he expects response. He expects commitment. Mary said, "Let it be with me according to your word." Are you saying that to God right now? "I just can't," you may be thinking. "I'm not able to make that kind of commitment." No, you aren't. You are no more able than I am to live up to the kind of submission and commitment God requires of us. But I remind you of what Gabriel said to Mary just before she made her expression of faith: "Nothing will be impossible with God."

Endnotes

1. <http://www.homileticsonline.com/Installments/nov2893.htm>, p. 2.

2. Harry Eskew, "O land of rest, for thee I sigh!" *Handbook to the Baptist Hymnal* (Nashville: Convention, 1992), pp. 204-205.

3. Lamar Williamson, Jr., *Mark*, Interpretation Commentary (Atlanta: John Knox, 1983), p. 242.

4. Both illustrations found at <http://www.homileticsonline.com/Installments/nov2893.htm>, p. 7.

5. All information and quotes about the Foundation are drawn from their website, <www.longnow.org>.

6. All information about the Doomsday Clock is drawn from the website of the *Bulletin of the Atomic Scientists*, <www.bullatomsci.org/doomsday.html>.

7. Philip Yancey, *What's So Amazing About Grace?* (Grand Rapids: Zondervan, 1997), p. 179.

8. Daniel W. Whittle, "Why Not Now?" in public domain.

9. Henry van Dyke, *The Story of the Other Wise Man* (New York: Ballantine, 1984).

10. Cyrus S. Nusbaum, "His Way With Thee," in public domain.

Part Three

Advent Imperatives

Watch!

Mark 13:24-37; 1 Corinthians 1:3-9

Mark 13 speaks to those who expect too much and to those who expect too little. It is especially pertinent for those who have forgotten to expect anything at all.[1]

The season of Advent is the season of expectancy. With the passing of Thanksgiving things start churning just beneath the surface and soon now they'll burst out all over the place. "Hurry, Christmas, hurry fast," the Chipmunks sing, and we know what they mean. At least we used to know what they mean. I guess that this is one of those times when we can learn something from our children. They can't wait for Christmas to get here and they feed off that energy in such a way that it inspires those of us who are around them. The anticipation of children regarding Christmas is contagious.

How expectant are we of the coming of Jesus? Do we have an anticipation that is so real that it is contagious? The season of Advent is the season of expectancy and that expectancy can and should branch off in three tributaries. First, we expectantly await the celebration of the coming of the Christ Child to Bethlehem's manger. Second, we expectantly await the coming of Christ into our lives in new and unexpected ways. Third, we expectantly await the coming again of Christ when he comes "in clouds with great power and glory" to "gather his elect from the four winds, from the ends of the earth to the ends of heaven" (Mark 13:26-27). The third expectation is what I want us to focus on. My, what a difference such expectation should make.

The fact is that Jesus will return some day. The further fact is that we can't know when that will be. Logic dictates that his return is closer now than it has ever been. The Bible dictates that we are always to be watching for and expecting his return. Our expectation, however, is not to be characterized by inactive waiting. Jesus' little parable makes that clear. He said that the coming of the Son of Man is like a man leaving his home to go on a trip. When he goes, he leaves his servants in charge and gives each one his work to do. He furthermore tells the doorkeeper to be on the watch. He then ends with those powerful words: "What I say to you I say to all: Watch" (13:37). What should characterize our watching for the return of our Lord?

We Watch In Hope

We forget sometimes that the New Testament's words about the return of Christ are words of good news for Christians. The return of Christ is our "blessed hope," it is something that we long for and look forward to. Why? Because in his return everything will be made as it ought to be. God's creation will finally fulfill its potential. Our lives will finally be whole and full. God's purposes will finally be fulfilled. The loving, peaceful, and gracious ways of Christ will finally be vindicated. Everything will be fulfilled and God himself will fulfill it. Hungers will be fulfilled, longings will be satisfied, questions will be answered, frustrations will be ended, and conflicts will be resolved.

We often say that we live in an age that needs hope and that is certainly the case. Even in the strongest and richest nation in the world we live with threats of terror and prospects of war hanging over our heads. Within this strongest and richest nation on earth live many who don't have enough food to eat or decent clothes to wear or access to a decent education. People need hope and we are to be taking that hope to them. But it is incorrect to say that we who are Christians need hope. We have hope. We have the greatest hope in the world. Maybe we forget sometimes or maybe we let circumstances push it way down deep inside us, but we are the carriers of hope. We watch in hope, not in futility. We know that Christ is going to return.

We Watch In Faithfulness

We are the servants who have been left behind while our Master is away. There is much work to be done in the meantime. It is our calling to share the love of Christ with all the people around us. It is our calling to live Christlike lives in the world, lives characterized by obedience, by love, by grace, and by faith. We have a tremendous calling to which we are to be faithful, and the only time we have to be faithful is right now. Today is all we have and we must be faithful in it. We are to be faithful in the disciplines of the faith and faithful in the work of the Lord.

Sometimes, though, we err on the side of caution. We are so aware of the dangers that we face in the world that we spend all our energy guarding against them and wishing that Jesus would come back and get us out of this mess. Other times we err on the side of a lack of caution. That is, we are so involved in doing what we do for the Lord that we don't take adequate care of our own spirits and we get blindsided by temptation or we let ourselves dry up.

A good model for how we are to live in the world while we wait is offered in the book of Nehemiah. Nehemiah was governor of Judah during the years after the return from Babylonian Exile. His main priority was to rebuild the wall around Jerusalem. It was hard work but it had to be done. To make matters worse, the people were under constant threat from enemies. What did Nehemiah lead them to do? He assigned half the people to work and half to stand guard. The builders always wore a sword. Some worked with a tool in one hand and a weapon in the other. The point is that they were defensive and offensive at the same time; they guarded themselves and did their work at the same time. So it should be with us. Let's watch for our Lord by guarding our souls but also by doing the work that is before us to do.

We Watch In Dependence

We do none of what I have talked about in our own strength or in our own ability. As Paul reminded the Corinthians at the beginning of his letter to them, God has given us all we need to be what he has called us to be. He said to them, "You are not lacking in any spiritual gift as you wait for the revealing of our Lord Jesus Christ"

(1 Corinthians 1:7). *So we are dependent on his empowerment of us to do the work to which he has called us.* We depend not on our own resources but rather on his.

We are also dependent on his sustenance; Paul said that Jesus Christ "will strengthen you to the end, so that you may be blameless on the day of our Lord Jesus Christ" (v. 8). We are not to anticipate the coming of Christ and the judgment to follow with fear and anxiety, not if we are his children. And, we are not to live in fear of failure or of falling. Rather we are to depend on the sustaining power of the Lord to enable us to persevere until the end. Then we will stand before him and be declared blameless not because of what we have done but because of what Christ has done. In his strength we really can become more and more like he intends for us to be. He will help us to become more mature and he will sustain us to the end.

We are also dependent on his faithfulness. That is, God is faithful to us. We are called to be faithful to him and sometimes we succeed and sometimes we don't. But always God is faithful to us. He saved us and he will be faithful to us. He has established his covenant with us and he will be faithful to it. His love will never end and his care for us will never die.

Conclusion

We are watching for Christ this Advent. We are watching for him to come to our lives in new and unexpected ways. We are watching for his arrival in Bethlehem's manger, but we are also watching for him to return in power and glory, and we watch knowing that will make all the difference. Knowing that will make all the difference now. Let us watch in hope, in faithfulness, and in dependence. Our waiting will not be in vain. Our Lord will come. Even so, come, Lord Jesus.

Repent!

Mark 1:1-8; 2 Peter 3:8-15a

A new beginning is a valuable thing. A fresh start is a great relief. On the second Sunday in Advent we hear the call to repent. The good news is that you can repent. You can have a fresh start. You have the chance for a new beginning.

When I was in seminary one of the television stations aired a brief devotional just before they played the National Anthem and signed off. (This was before the invention of infomercials and the arrival of all-night television.) One of my professors mentioned that the station was glad to use students and so I called them up. The next thing I knew I was down at the television station with my suit on preparing to film a week's worth of devotions. The first six went smoothly. On the seventh, though, I lost my rhythm and stumbled over some of the words. I asked in apologetic tones, "May I start that one over?" The young lady operating the camera said, "Sure, it's no problem." Then she said, "Do you ever watch our newscast?" "Yes," I replied. "Well," she said, "you know those editorials that our general manager does? We have to do those things at least ten times every week before he can get it right." I was grateful for the chance to start over that one time. I guess that maybe the general manager was ten times as grateful as I was. It's nice to be able just to rewind the tape and start over, erasing what we messed up and putting something better in its place.

I don't think that the image of rewinding a tape and starting over is an adequate metaphor for repentance. It works in some ways. When God forgives our sins, they are gone for good in the sense that we will not be judged for them. That does not mean, however, that it is all somehow easy and painless and trivial. It does not mean that we just say, "I'm sorry," and go on about our merry way. True repentance means much more than that.

Real repentance cannot happen unless God himself has paved the way. God is the instigator of repentance. John the Baptist came as the precursor to the Messiah. He was a player in the culmination of what God had been doing throughout the history of humankind. He preached repentance because his role was to prepare the way for the Savior. The people were able to hear and to respond to his message of repentance because he stood in the tradition of the great Old Testament prophets — he looked like Elijah, he fulfilled the prophecies of Isaiah and Malachi, and he sounded like any number of prophets. We can repent because God has always been about the business of offering the opportunity for repentance.

For another thing, real repentance leads to real change. This truth is basic to the meaning of the word. The Greek word means to change the mind but behind it lies the Hebrew concept of turning around and going the other way. So to repent is to have not only your mind changed but also to have your life changed. How does such repentance come about?

First, we acknowledge and tell the truth about ourselves. The people who came to John were "confessing their sins" (Mark 1:5). Repentance can only take place when we are honest about the fact that we are sinners and we acknowledge that fact before God.

Second, we participate in what God is doing to forgive our sins. The people came submitting themselves for baptism. Now, the act of baptism does not, in and of itself, constitute forgiveness. It is very important, however, because it does communicate forgiveness. It says to us in a powerful way that we have been forgiven because we have participated in what God is doing to save us. This is even more meaningful to us than it would have been to those whom John baptized. Why? Because we live on this side of the death and burial and resurrection of Jesus and so we realize that we are, in our baptism, buried with Christ and raised to new life in him.

Third, we come to know the indwelling power of God. John said that he baptized folks with water, but that the coming one would baptize with the Holy Spirit. The Holy Spirit is the very presence and power of God with us in our daily lives. Jesus Christ was Immanuel, "God with us," while he was on the earth, and the Holy Spirit is "God with us" in an ongoing way. The Spirit continuously communicates to us that we belong to God and teaches us what we need to know about God. The Spirit equips us and inspires us to live as forgiven people who are growing in sanctification even in this sin-besotted world. God is with us. The news can't get much better than that.

So who needs to repent? We all do. Some of us have never repented at all. If you have not acknowledged the fact that you are a sinner and have never turned to God and asked for his forgiveness, you need to repent. Those of us who are followers of Christ all fall under the heading of those who have a long way to go. We are still beset by our prejudices, by our habits, by our attitudes that reflect the mind of the world rather than the mind of Christ, by our addictions, by our shallow or faulty motives, by our judgmentalism, by our legalism, and by our lack of discipline. We need to repent.

But we need to tell the truth about our limitations. In John's day people repented when John told them that they needed to do so to prepare for the coming Messiah. Peter wrote to his audience that they needed to see the time before Christ returned as an opportunity to repent. "The Lord is coming, so repent." It is a compelling summons. But let's tell the truth about ourselves. During the holiday season we often find ourselves expecting guests. We know they're coming; we even know *when* they are coming. So what do we do? We get busy putting our house in order. We do everything we can to make it spic-and-span and impressive. It's all temporary, though. They know and we know that once the visit is over everything will go back to its normal state, which is probably somewhere between a little messy and totally chaotic.

Such is life, but such is not how repentance is supposed to be. It is not enough to say, "Jesus may come back at any minute and so I have to get my life straightened out." Such an approach is ineffective because once we stop thinking about it, or we get distracted by something else, things will just return to normal. It is not enough to spruce up just in case Jesus returns soon. Our repentance and our increasing holiness should be based on what is real and what is vital. What is real and vital is the fact that because Christ came, because he continues to come, and because he will come again, we have the chance for a new beginning. John Stendahl put that glorious good news this way: "To be at a beginning is to find that we are not prisoners of the past."[2] Christ will do a new thing in you, perhaps starting with a brand new beginning today or perhaps building on what he has already done in your life. You needn't be a prisoner to what you have done or what you have been in the past. Instead you can accept God's offer of a chance to repent — to be changed, to be transformed. You can, from this moment on, become more and more like Christ. You can constantly become more and more loving toward God and toward other people. Love will be central to what you will be becoming, because love is the one thing in life that never ends.[3]

Rejoice!

Psalm 126; 1 Thessalonians 5:16-24

I keep coming back to it time after time, so it is never going to stop being one of the most significant passages in the Bible for me. It is found in the otherwise rather obscure book of Habakkuk:

> *Though the fig tree does not blossom,*
> *and no fruit is on the vines;*
> *though the produce of the olive fails*
> *and the fields yield no food;*
> *though the flock is cut off from the fold*
> *and there is no herd in the stalls,*
> *yet I will rejoice in the LORD;*
> *I will exult in the God of my salvation.*
> — Habakkuk 3:17-18

The passage reminds us of a significant issue that we will not think about until circumstances force us to consider it. The issue is this: How can we know joy even in the midst of the worst that life can throw at us? I am not implying that we necessarily and automatically know joy in the best of times. Many people just kind of float through and hope for the best, never really tapping into the joy that Christ makes possible in our lives. During Advent, as we draw ever closer and closer to Christmas, we need to be told or to be reminded that because of Christmas, real joy is possible.

Someone has said that the early church knew what it was doing when it set the date for our Christmas observance on December 25.[4] I think he's right. After all, look at what's been happening lately. The darkness of night has been coming upon us earlier and earlier. The weather has been gray and damp and cold. Such atmospherics can push our spirits down and cause us to forget that the light and life of spring are just around the corner. In the midst of such potential depression, the church stands up and insists that our world be reminded of this great truth: "Joy to the world! The Lord is come!" We light the candles and we turn on the lights and we sing the songs and we tell the good news that Jesus Christ is born. Into the midst of darkness we shine the *light of the world* and we insist that he really does make all the difference. We insist that the "good tidings of great joy" are not only for all people but are also for all situations and for all circumstances, no matter what is happening. We insist that we celebrate Christmas because Christ came, because he continues to come, and because he will come again. We insist that his coming brings joy. Because of Christ, and only because of Christ, we can "rejoice always" and we can "give thanks in all circumstances" (1 Thessalonians 5:16, 18a).

That means that we rejoice in the here and now no matter what the here and now brings. We know that one day our joy will be complete when we all get to heaven; we know that our joy will be fulfilled when Christ returns. But, Paul tells us that we are to "rejoice always" and to "give thanks in all circumstances" as we live these lives.

Joy and sorrow are companions in our lives. To say that because of Christ we have joy is not to say that we don't have sorrow. But we can say that because of Christ even our sorrows have meaning and that our joys have final sway. John Goldingay is a British professor who, after many years of teaching in England, moved to California to teach at Fuller Theological Seminary. His wife, Ann, has lived for many years with multiple sclerosis and just before they moved to California she lost her ability to walk. Goldingay published a book about their experiences that included the following words:

> *Then there was an occasion when I was running around our sports field feeling joyful at 7:45 a.m. It was the day I was to take Ann to the rehabilitation center for a stay.... Yet, as I was putting her into the car I found myself crying, and I knew it was because that sort of moment brings home to me the reality of her illness. Whereas we try to live a "normal" life, a moment like that reminds me of the sadness of how things actually are. That did not surprise me. What did surprise me was that juxtaposition of joy and tears. It should not have surprised me, because that is how our life is and*

> *how most human life is, I suspect. Quite often joy alternates with sadness. "Weeping may remain for a night, but rejoicing comes in the morning" (Psalm 30:5).*[5]

We live with joy and sorrow mingled together. That is the way we live, with childish laughter mixed with traces of sorrow. But the incarnation and crucifixion and resurrection of Christ teach us that God is in it all.

Joseph Cardinal Bernardin, toward the end of his life, reflected on the events of his last few years. He knew that he was dying. He was falsely accused of the sexual abuse of a seminarian. He was then diagnosed with pancreatic cancer. Surgery and treatment seemed to go well, but he was later diagnosed with the liver cancer that would prove terminal. Toward the end of his life, he wrote of how he had experienced good and bad together during his struggles. He wrote of his experiences to demonstrate "how the good and the bad are always present in our human condition and, that if we 'let go,' if we place ourselves totally in the hands of the Lord, the good will prevail."[6] That is why we can give thanks in all circumstances. God can write straight with crooked lines. If we let go and trust God, as the great old Christmas hymn says, "The wrong will fail, the right prevail."

Even as the First Advent of Christ calls us backward and the Second Advent of Christ calls us forward, we must realize that it is the presence of Christ right now that enables us to have joy right now. But to experience that joy we must be willing to live in the moment and to see how the things that are happening can turn our lives in wonderful ways that we would never have anticipated.

Marion Ettlinger is a photographer who is known for her portraits of authors. She once spoke about an experience she had when, as a young photographer, she was assigned by *Esquire* magazine to photograph Truman Capote. It did not go well. Even though she was there on the right day, he thought she was there on the wrong one. He wouldn't let her in his house. He was wearing an old sweatshirt. Finally he said that if she was going to shoot any pictures, she needed to start right then. So she began snapping photographs of him glaring at her. She then asked him to turn so that she could shoot him in profile. He did, and he began to raise his chin. After she shot a few like that he said that the shoot was over and he went back inside. The pictures are quite impressive. Ettlinger said that prior to her difficult experience with Capote, she assumed that a good result depended on the cooperation of the subject. But, she said, "He taught me that that's not necessarily true and that if you go with what's happening, something much more interesting and more beautiful might happen as a result of that."[7]

That is a marvelous picture of how to live a life that is full of joy. Live in the moment. Be willing to abandon your plans. Know that control is of limited value. Go with what's happening, with what God is working out in your life, with the ways in which God will write straight with crooked lines, and in Christ your life will be filled with joy.

Worship!

Luke 1:26-56

"My soul magnifies the Lord," Mary said, and I think that she meant it. I also think that it is hard for us to put ourselves in Mary's place or to imagine that the same responses made by Mary are responses that could be made by us. But if you think about it, it is fair to say that Jesus comes to us, too, and that is why Mary's soul magnified the Lord: because Jesus had come to her. The coming of Jesus to us inspires us to worship and praise God.

I believe that the main thing about the coming of Jesus to us that should inspire our praise is what it teaches us about the grace of God. We know of no merit on Mary's part that caused God to choose her. In fact, it is exactly because God chose Mary despite her absence of merit that makes it such an act of grace. We see Mary's awareness of her status in several places. When Gabriel said "Greetings, favored one! The Lord is with you," Mary wondered what in the world that could be all about (vv. 28-29). In her song she said, "My spirit rejoices in God my Savior, for he has looked with favor on the lowliness of his servant" (vv. 47-48). God chooses and uses the humble and lowly exactly because they are humble and lowly. He chooses those who are undeserving exactly because they are undeserving. "Blessed are the poor in spirit," the baby who was born to Mary would say after he grew up. He meant then, and still means now, that God can bless and use those who realize their insufficiency and their utter dependence on God.

Carlo Carretto has said, " 'He has regarded the lowliness of his handmaiden,' said Mary when she saw, accepting her nothingness, the essential love of God and felt her flesh become the dwelling place and nourishment of the word incarnate. How wonderful that Mary's nothingness should attract God's all."[8] Indeed. How wonderful that our nothingness should attract God's all. Jesus has come to us, has been born in us, has come to live in us. The very Son of God has chosen to dwell in us despite, or maybe because of, our nothingness. What can we do other than worship the God who has shown us that kind of grace?

In his gracious acts toward us, God shows his power. Christmas is, as is all the story of Jesus and his church, all about what God has done, is doing, and will do. When Mary asked her very good question about how she could bear a son when she was a virgin, the answer she received was all about God: "The Holy Spirit will come upon you, and the power of the Most High will overshadow you; therefore the child to be born will be holy; he will be called Son of God.... For nothing will be impossible with God" (vv. 35, 37). Make no mistake about it: We praise and worship God because of what he has done, because of how he has shown and continues to show his power. We experience that power in our own lives and we see how his power operates in the lives of other people. His power elicits our praise.

But what does it mean to worship God for all the wonderful and gracious things that he has done and is doing? Surely it means to do what we gather as the church to do: It means to sing, rejoice, and celebrate as the body of Christ. But it means something else. It means to share in what God is doing. It means to participate in what God is doing. It means to become a part of what God is doing. It means to live our lives in service to him. Mary was worshiping God when she sang in response to what he had done. But she was also worshiping God when she said, "Here am I, the servant of the Lord; let it be with me according to your word" (v. 38). She willingly submitted to how the Lord wanted to use her in carrying out his plan of salvation.

Such willingness and such submission are part of our worship of God, and it can be very hard to worship that way. As Conrad Hyers has said, "The 'chosen' of God are clearly not chosen on the basis of having the most to offer, but rather on the basis of having nothing to offer but themselves. And the 'reward' of this chosenness is often that of being the clown, the scapegoat, the butt of the joke, the 'fool for Christ's sake.' "[9] Mary had to become a fool for Christ's sake. She had to become the butt of the joke for Christ's sake. She immediately left town upon the reception of her good news. No doubt but that her situation set the tongues of Nazareth wagging, especially those that belonged to the polite and the respectable and the other hypocrites. But that's the way God works. He chooses the foolish to shame the wise, the humble to shame the proud, and the weak to shame the powerful. God's ways are the reverse of the ways of the world, and he chooses the unexpected to do the unexpected in ways that are unexpected.

Are you submitting yourself to the will and ways of God in your own life? It is about what God is doing, but in some mysterious way it does matter whether or not we participate in it. Frederick Buechner, in his imaginative way, imagined what Gabriel might have been going through when he brought the good news to Mary.

> *She struck the angel Gabriel as hardly old enough to have a child at all, let alone this child, but he'd been entrusted with a message to give her, and he gave it.*
>
> *He told her what the child was to be named, and who he was to be, and something about the mystery that was to come upon her. "You mustn't be afraid, Mary," he said.*
>
> *As he said it, he only hoped she wouldn't notice that beneath the great, golden wings he himself was trembling with fear to think the whole future of creation hung now on the answer of a girl.*[10]

God was doing what God was doing, and in his grace he chose Mary. Somehow what she said next really mattered. Maybe what you say next really matters. Will we worship God for what he has done in Christ by submitting ourselves to the ways in which God wants to use us?

Endnotes

1. Lamar Williamson, Jr., *Mark*, Interpretation Commentary (Louisville: John Knox, 1983), p. 243.

2. John Stendahl, "On Your Mark," *Christian Century* (November 20-December 3, 2002), p. 16.

3. Paul Tillich, *The Shaking of the Foundations* (New York: Charles Scribner's Sons, 1948), p. 186.

4. Stephens G. Lytch, "We Can Rejoice," *The Minister's Manual 2002*, ed. James W. Cox (San Francisco: Jossey-Bass, 2001), p. 291.

5. John Goldingay, *Walk On: Life, Loss, Trust, and Other Realities* (Grand Rapids: Baker, 2002), pp. 98-99.

6. Joseph Cardinal Bernardin, *The Gift of Peace* (New York: Image, 1998), pp. xi-xiii.

7. As heard in an interview with Terry Gross on the radio program *Fresh Air* on December 12, 2002.

8. Carlo Carretto, *Letters from the Desert*, in "Reflections," *Christianity Today* (December 9, 2002), p. 53.

9. Conrad Hyers, "The Nativity as Divine Comedy," *Christian Century* (December 11, 1974), pp. 1168-1172.

10. Frederick Buechner, *Peculiar Treasures: A Biblical Who's Who* (San Francisco, HarperSanFranciso, 1979), p. 44. Used by permission.

www.ingramcontent.com/pod-product-compliance
Lightning Source LLC
Chambersburg PA
CBHW071743040426
42446CB00012B/2456